Sport Billy (the official mascot of FIFA) is the world's greatest athlete. He was sent down to Earth from the planet Olympus to cope with Vanda and her band of colourful villains. They are masters of disguise and try to sabotage sporting events and destroy the ideals of fair play.

Billy has tremendous sporting abilities and always plays the game without using his space powers. But when Vanda tries her treachery, Billy is allowed to call on the president of Olympus, Sportikus, for help and advice. Billy also has his Omnisac, a travel bag which can produce anything imaginable. Lilly, his girlfriend, and Willy, the dog, accompany Billy on his travels.

His four main aims are to fight violence and vandalism in sports and life; to promote fair play and the joy of practice in sports; to help to protect athletes while practising sports; and to promote health and weight consciousness among young people.

First Edition

© SPORT BILLY PRODUCTIONS MCMLXXXII
© LADYBIRD BOOKS LTD MCMLXXXII

SPORT BILLY

The Winning Goal

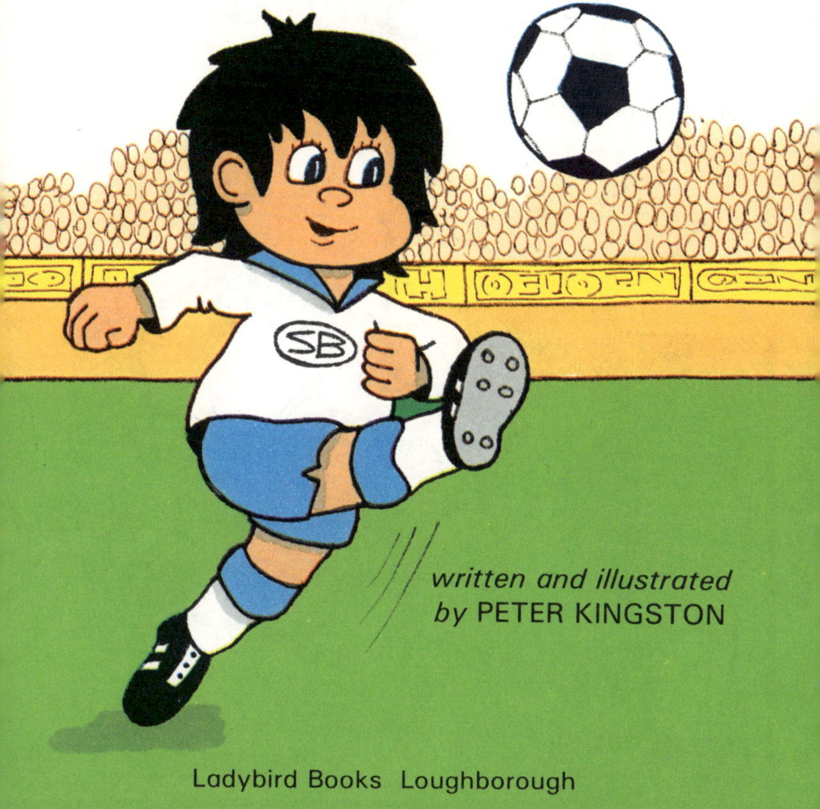

written and illustrated by PETER KINGSTON

Ladybird Books Loughborough

THE DAY BEFORE THE FOOTBALL FINAL, BILLY'S TEAM WERE PREPARING.....

4

LILLY AND WILLY ARRIVED AT THE STADIUM TO HELP THEM

MEANWHILE, IN A NEARBY HOTEL, VANDA'S TEAM WERE JUST BEING VERY LAZY

8

9

BILLY'S BOYS STARTED TO PRACTISE THEIR GOAL SCORING

BUT VANDA POINTED HER FINGER AT THE BALL AND....

12

CRACK!! IT WAS AS HARD AS STONE!

OH DEAR! THAT'S ONE MAN LESS IN THE TEAM

THE BOYS CONTINUED PRACTISING.....

...AND ONCE AGAIN, VANDA POINTED THAT FINGER

CRUNCH!! SUDDENLY THE GROUND SPLIT OPEN AND TWO OF BILLY'S MEN FELL DOWN

18

MASCOT!! I WISH THEY WOULD LET ME PLAY!!

BACK TO THE FIELD, LADS. MORE PRACTICE!!

SATURDAY ARRIVED. THE STADIUM WAS PACKED WITH FANS. EVERYBODY WAITED EXCITEDLY AS THE BAND MARCHED OFF

THE VANDALS CAME OUT AND EVERYBODY BOOED

BUT THEY CHEERED AS BILLY'S TEAM APPEARED

WELL, AS THEIR MASCOT, I'D BETTER BARK LOUDLY

THE TIME HAD COME.
THE REFEREE STARTED THE BIG MATCH

BILLY'S TEAM RAN CIRCLES AROUND THE VANDALS, WHO DID NOT SEEM TO BE VERY FIT

BUT AS THE WELL-AIMED BALL SPED TOWARDS THE GOAL, IT JUST WHIZZED AWAY —

AND AGAIN, AND AGAIN AND...

WHATEVER IS GOING ON !!! WHY IS THE BALL ACTING SO STRANGELY?

I DON'T KNOW, BILLY, BUT THEIR TEAM HAS JUST SCORED A GOAL!

BEFORE BILLY'S TEAM COULD FIGHT BACK, IT WAS HALF-TIME

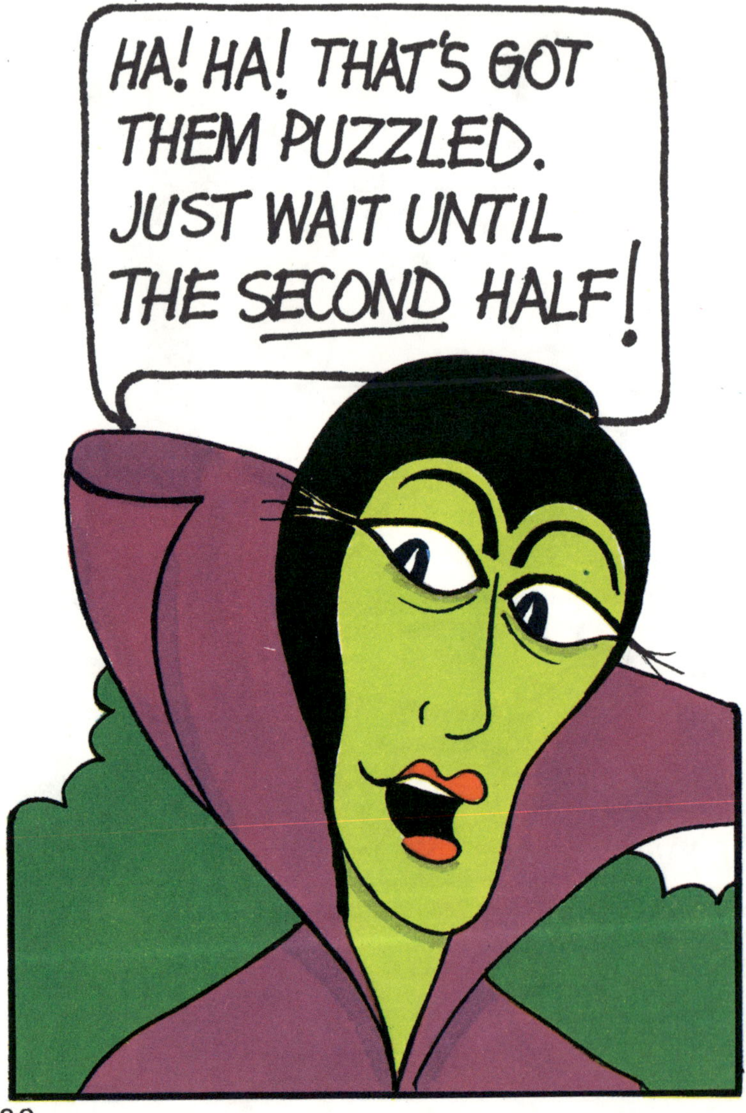
HA! HA! THAT'S GOT THEM PUZZLED. JUST WAIT UNTIL THE SECOND HALF!

BILLY WANDERED OUTSIDE TO TRY AND SORT OUT A PLAN OF ACTION
I'LL CALL UP PRESIDENT SPORTIKUS AND SEE IF HE CAN HELP

YES, IT'S IN MY OMNISAC. BUT I HAVEN'T ANY PLURANIUM LEFT AT ALL!

PRESIDENT SPORTICUS QUICKLY SWITCHED ON ALL HIS COMPUTERS TO FIND THE NEAREST PLURANIUM SUPPLIER

34

BILLY DASHED BACK INTO THE DRESSING ROOM

GRABBED HIS OMNISAC AND . . . .

HEY, BILLY WHERE ARE YOU GOING?

OH, I WON'T BE MORE THAN FIVE MINUTES

THERE'S THE PLACE. I'LL LAND AT THE BACK

HE LANDED BEHIND THE BUILDING AND DASHED TO THE DOOR....

BILLY QUICKLY EXPLAINED . . . . .

HERE, BILLY. IT'S MY LAST BOX OF PLURANIUM

THANKS A LOT. I MUST HURRY NOW . . . .

I'VE ONLY GOT TWO MINUTES TO GET BACK

IN JUST HALF A MINUTE HE WAS BACK

I'LL JUST POP THE JET BACK AND GET MY GUN

BILLY QUICKLY TOOK OFF HIS TRACK SUIT AND WAS READY TO PLAY. HE HID THE PLURANIUM GUN OUT OF SIGHT

BILLY'S TEAM WENT OUT ONTO THE PITCH

NOW WE'LL WIN THIS MATCH. YOU'LL SEE!

JUST AHEAD NOBODY NOTICED VANDA DISGUISED AS A PHOTOGRAPHER

NOW TO MAKE SURE MY TEAM WILL WIN

JUST BEFORE KICK-OFF, BILLY QUICKLY AIMED HIS PLURANIUM GUN AND....

THE WHISTLE BLEW AND THE GAME STARTED

BILLY'S TEAM WERE PLAYING WELL AND SOON HAD THE CHANCE TO SCORE. NOW IT WAS 1-1

THE FINAL WHISTLE BLEW. THE GAME WAS OVER

HOORAY!!
WE'VE WON